TRADITIONAL MALTESE CATHOLIC LENTEN COOKBOOK

HOPE AND LIFE PRESS (Ed.)

First published in 2019 by
HOPE AND LIFE PRESS

Traditional Maltese Catholic Lenten Cookbook

ISBN 978-17928691-2-9 paperback edition.

Copyright © 2019 Hope and Life Press – All rights reserved.

Published by
HOPE AND LIFE PRESS

Distributed by
PANORMI BOOKS
panormibooks.com

All rights reserved. No part of this work may be reproduced, stored in a retrieval system, or submitted in any form or by any means, electronic, mechanical, photocopying, recording or otherwise, without the prior written permission of the publisher. This book may not be lent, resold, hired out or otherwise disposed of by way of trade in any form of binding or cover other than that in which it is published, without the prior written consent of the publishers.

Printed in the United States of America.

Contents

Traditional Maltese Catholic Lenten Cookbook
1. Soups
    1.1. Fish Soup / *Aljotta* — 5
    1.2. Maltese Vegetable Soup / *Minestra tal-Ħaxix* — 6
    1.3. Mediterranean Soup / *Soppa Mediterranja* — 7
    1.4. Potato Soup / *Soppa tal-Patata* — 8
    1.5. Pumpkin Soup / *Soppa tal-Qargħa Aħmar* — 9
    1.6. Widow's Soup / *Soppa tal-Armla* — 10
2. Dips
    2.1. Bean Paste / *Bigilla* — 11
3. Breads
    3.1. Apostles Unleavened Bagel / *Qagħqa tal-Appostli* — 12
    3.2. Maltese Bread / *Ħobż Malti* — 13
    3.3. Lenten Flatbread / *Ftira tar-Randan* — 14
4. Main Dishes
    4.1. Artichokes Stew / *Stuffat tal-Qaqoċċ* — 15
    4.2. Cauliflower Pie / *Torta tal-Pastard* — 17
    4.3. Couscous with Broad Beans / *Kusksu bil-Ful* — 19
    4.4. Mahi-Mahi Pie / *Torta tal-Lampuki* — 20
    4.5. Fried Cabbage with Eggs / *Kaboċċi Moqlija bil-Bajd* — 21
    4.6. Maltese Scrambled Eggs / *Balbuljata* — 22
    4.7. Octopus / *Qarnita* — 23
    4.8. Spaghetti with Anchovies / *Spagetti bl-Inċova* — 24
    4.9. Spaghetti with Octopus / *Spagetti bil-Qarnit* — 25
    4.10 Spinach and Tuna Pie / *Torta tat-Tonn u l-Ispinaċi* — 27
    4.11 Spinach Lasagna / *Lażanja tal-Ispinaċi* — 28
    4.12 Stuffed Green Peppers / *Bżar Aħdar Ikkuppat* — 29
    4.13 Stuffed Green Peppers with Mahi-Mahi / *Bżar Aħdar Ikkuppat bil-Lampuki* — 31
    4.14 Stuffed Green Peppers with Tuna / *Bżar Aħdar bit-Tonn taż-Żejt* — 32

	4.15 Stuffed Marrows / *Qargħa Bagħli Kkuppat*	33
	4.16 Tuna Fish Stew / *Stuffat tat-Tonn*	34
	4.17 Fried Vermicelli Pie / *Tarja bil-Bajd*	35
5.	DRINKS	
	5.1. Carob Syrup / *Ġulepp*	36
	5.2. Honeyed Wine / *Imbid bl-Għasel*	37
	5.3. Maltese Coffee / *Kafè Malti Msajjar*	38
6.	PUDDINGS	
	6.1. Rice Pudding / *Pudina tar-Ross*	39
7.	DESSERTS	
	7.1. Deep Fried Dates / *Imqaret*	40
	7.2. Hard Carob Sweets / *Karamelli tal-Ħarrub*	42
	7.3. Hot Cross Buns	43
	7.4. *Kwareżimal*	45
	7.5. Maltese Nougat / *Qubbajt*	47
	7.6. Treacle Rings / *Qagħaq tal-Għasel*	48
8.	COOKIES	
	8.1. Bitter Almond Biscuits / *Biskuttini tal-Lewż Morr*	50
	8.2. Crunchy Maltese Rusks / *Biskuttelli*	51
	8.3. Hard Thin Biscuits / *Galletti*	52
	8.4. Village Biscuits / *Biskuttini tar-Raħal*	53
9.	EASTER FARE	
	9.1. Rabbit with Vermouth / *Fenek bil-Vermut*	54
	9.2. Almonds Pie / *Torta tal-Lewż*	56
	9.3. Shaped Almonds Easter Cake / *Figolla tal-Għid*	57
	9.4. Saint Joseph's Fritters / *Zeppoli ta' San Ġużepp*	59

1 – Soups

Fish Soup
Aljotta

Ingredients
450g (16oz) white fish[1]
2 onions chopped
12 garlic cloves minced
450g (16oz) tomatoes peeled and sliced
1 tsp tomato paste
1 tsp olive oil
pinch of marjoram and dry mint
5 peppercorns
½ cup cooked rice
4 cups fish stock
salt and pepper

Method
1. Fry the chopped onion in olive oil until soft.
2. Add the garlic, herbs, and tomato paste. Cook for a few minutes.
3. Add the tomatoes and fish stock. Bring everything to a boil.
4. Add the fish, bring to a boil, and simmer for about 10 minutes.
5. Add the cooked rice. Sprinkle the salt and pepper, and serve.

---

[1] Preferably the head of the fish for better flavor.

Maltese Vegetable Soup
Minestra tal-Ħaxix

Ingredients

2 marrows
4 potatoes
2 onions
400g (14oz) pumpkin
1 small cabbage
1 small cauliflower
2 turnips
2 tomatoes
2 carrots
1 tsp tomato purée
200g (7oz) small-shaped pasta
750ml (25.36fl oz) water
salt and pepper
Parmesan cheese grated

Method

1. Chop the vegetables and place them in a pot. Add the water, tomato purée, and season.
2. Bring to a boil and let the pot simmer until the vegetables are tender. Then add a spoonful of olive oil.
3. Add the pasta and keep simmering until the pasta is done.
4. Sprinkle salt and pepper. Serve with a dollop of parmesan cheese.

Mediterranean Soup
Soppa Mediterranja

Ingredients
2 tbsp olive oil
1 leek sliced thin
2 garlic cloves crushed
2 celery sticks sliced
230g (8oz) mushrooms
550g (19.5oz) tomato purée
570ml (20fl oz) vegetable stock
425g (15oz) mixed beans
230g (8oz) pasta
salt and pepper

Garnish
30g (1oz) toasted cashew nuts
30g (1oz) olives
3 tbsp fresh coriander chopped
grated Parmesan cheese

Method
1. Cook the vegetables in heated olive oil for 5 minutes in a heavy pan, stirring as needed.
2. Add the tomato purée and vegetable stock. Bring to a boil.
3. Stir everything well and add the pasta, simmering for about 7 minutes. Stir frequently while the pasta is cooking to prevent it from sticking.
4. Season to taste with salt and pepper. Spoon into warmed soup bowls.
5. Place the garnish in separate bowls and serve.

Potato Soup
Soppa tal-Patata

<u>Ingredients</u>
medium-sized potatoes peeled and sliced
2 carrots diced
¼ cup parsley chopped
5 celery stalks diced
2 l (68fl oz) water
1 onion chopped
5 tbsp butter
5 tbsp flour
1.5 cups milk
salt and pepper

<u>Method</u>
1. Cook the potatoes, carrots, parsley, and celery in water until tender, in a large pan, for about 20 minutes.
2. Drain and reserve the liquid, setting the vegetables aside.
3. In the same pan, sauté the onion in butter until soft.
4. Stir in the flour, salt and pepper. Add the milk, stirring constantly until the mixture is thick.
5. Stir in the cooked vegetables.
6. Add 1 cup or more of the reserved cooking liquid until the soup is of the desired consistency.
7. Spoon into warm soup bowls and serve.

Pumpkin Soup
Soppa tal-Qargħ'Aħmar

Ingredients
1 large onion chopped
2 tbsp olive oil
125g (5oz) tomato purée
700g (25oz) pumpkin peeled and diced
75g (3oz) semolina
1 l (34fl oz) boiling water
grated Parmesan cheese
salt and pepper
bread

Method
1. Heat the oil and fry the chopped onion. Then add in the tomato purée and the diced pumpkin.
2. Fry everything gently for 5 minutes, stirring continuously.
3. Add the boiling water, salt and pepper. Simmer until the pumpkin is well-cooked.
4. Mash in the vegetables by hand.
5. Add the semolina gently to avoid lumping and cook on low heat for 9 minutes. Spoon into warm soup bowls and serve.
6. Toast the bread and cut it into small cubes. Serve warm and separately like the Parmesan cheese.

Widow's Soup
Soppa tal-Armla

Ingredients

100g (4oz) onions
100g (4oz) potatoes
100g (4oz) zucchini
150g (5.3oz) tomatoes peeled
200g (8oz) ricotta cheese
125g (4.5oz) peas
125g (4.5oz) cauliflower
50g (2oz) tomato paste
4 eggs boiled
4 goat's cheeselets (*ġbejniet bojod*)
salt and pepper

Method
1. Slice the vegetables and fry the onions.
2. Add all the ingredients into a pot except for the eggs, ricotta, and cheeselets.
3. Season everything with salt and pepper. Bring to a boil.
4. Simmer the above mix until the vegetables are well-cooked.
5. Cut the ricotta into large chunks and add, together with the boiled eggs.
6. Add the cheeselets and serve.

2 – Dips

Bean Paste
Bigilla

<u>Ingredients</u>
250g *ful tal-ġirba* (Djerba beans)
2 tbsp olive oil
1 head of garlic crushed
1 tbsp marjoram, mint, or basil
salt
olive oil

<u>Method</u>
1. Wash the brown beans and let them soak overnight in cold water.
2. Discard the water, then boil the beans until they become very tender and the water evaporates.
3. Mash the beans with a fork to obtain the best consistency and spoon the mixture into a large bowl.
4. Add in all the other ingredients and mix.
5. Add more olive oil on top and serve[2].

---

[2] Should be preferably eaten with Maltese bread for the appropriate traditional flavor.

3 – BREADS

Apostles Unleavened Bagel
Qagħqa tal-Appostli

Ingredients
500g (18oz) plain flour
100g (4oz) margarine
4 tsp yeast
100g (4oz) sugar
grated rind of 1 orange
grated rind of 1 lemon
2 tbsp caraway seeds
¼ tsp cloves
¼ tsp cinnamon
50gr citrus diced (*konfettura*)
1 tsp blossom water
1 tsp anisette
275ml (9.3fl oz) lukewarm water
4 tbsp sesame
50gr (2oz) almonds

Method
1. Sift the flour and margarine. Add the yeast, sugar, orange and lemon peel, caraway seeds, cloves, cinnamon, and diced citrus. Mix everything well together.
2. Add the blossom water, anisette, and lukewarm water. Make the dough and divide it in two. Use each part to make a ring of bread and put the almonds, evenly spaced, into its surface.
3. Wrap the bread in sesame and cook for about 30 minutes in a hot oven. Let the bread cool down and serve.

Maltese Bread
Ħobż Malti

Ingredients
600g (21oz) flour
10g (0.4oz) salt
15g (0.5oz) sugar
15g (0.5oz) margarine
25g (0.9oz) yeast
345ml (12fl oz) lukewarm water
1 tbsp milk

Method
1. Mix the flour, salt, and 13argarine. Add the yeast.
2. Mix the lukewarm water, sugar, and milk. Add onto the flour and knead this mixture until the dough is white and elastic.
3. Place in a bowl. Seal with cling film and a wet dishcloth.
4. Set the bowl to rest in a warm place for about 1 hour.
5. Work the dough, cutting into small pieces. Then place on a baking tray, paste them with egg, cut with a knife, and let the pieces rest for about 15 minutes.
6. Cook in an oven[3] at a temperature of 232°C (450°F), with gas mark 6-8, for about 15 minutes.
7. Remove the bread from the oven. Let it cool and serve.

---

[3] Maltese bread is best baked in a traditional wood oven to obtain the appropriate flavor.

Lenten Flatbread
Ftira tar-Randan

Ingredients
450g (16oz) plain flour
water as needed
salt to preference
yeast as needed
6 tbsp olive oil
6 tbsp honey

Method
1. Mix the flour, salt, yeast, and water in a large bowl until it turns into a dough. Cover and let it set for 30 minutes.
2. Shape the dough into 1/2 centimeter (0.2") thick rounds. Fry the rounds in a flat pan, in olive oil, until golden brown. Turn them over while frying.
3. Remove from the heat and drizzle the top of the bread rounds with a dash of honey. Serve warm.

4 – Main Dishes

Artichokes Stew
Stuffat tal-Qaqoċċ

Ingredients
4 large tender artichokes
4 small onions finely chopped
200g (7oz) broad beans
200g (7oz) peas
400g (14oz) fresh tomatoes
2 garlic cloves crushed
1 tbsp parsley
1 tbsp olive oil
1 goat's cheeselet (*ġbejna*)
2 eggs
lemon juice
salt and pepper

Method
1. Remove all the tough outer leaves of the artichokes. Then cut off the tops of the remaining leaves and remove the choke.
2. Cut the artichokes in half and place them in a bowl covered in watered lemon juice.
3. Heat the olive oil in a saucepan and fry the chopped onions until they are soft.
4. Add the garlic. As soon as it turns golden, add the tomatoes. Bring to a boil, then add the parsley, salt and pepper.
5. Lower the temperature and add the artichoke hearts. When these are almost done, add the broad beans and peas, stirring gently. Add a little water as needed to make sure all the vegetables are immersed.

6. Continue simmering and stirring until the vegetables are tender.
7. Add the eggs and goat's cheeselet into a hollow you make with a wooden spoon.
8. As soon as the eggs are poached, serve the stew hot.

Cauliflower Pie
Torta tal-Pastard

Ingredients
short crust pastry
800g (28.2oz) cauliflower
1 tbsp butter
3 eggs
grated Parmesan cheese
parsley finely chopped
salt and pepper

White Sauce
25g (1oz) margarine
25g (1oz) flour
300ml (10fl oz) milk
1 onion

Method
1. Clean and rinse the cauliflower, then place it in a deep pan and cover it with water. Add the salt and bring to a boil until it is cooked.
2. Drain the water and let the cauliflower rest until cooled down.
3. On a low flame melt the margarine in a pan, then add the chopped onion. Stir gently until they are both golden brown.
4. Add the flour, continuously stirring, while adding the milk a little at a time, until it becomes thick and creamy. Then remove from the heat.
5. Mash the cauliflower, add the white sauce, salt and pepper, grated cheese, and eggs. Mix them well.
6. Melt the butter in a flan dish and cover it with the short crust pastry. Add the cauliflower mixture, covering the base.

7. Add the grated cheese and parsley on top of the cauliflower mix.
8. Cook in a moderate oven for 40 minutes until the top is golden. Serve hot.

Couscous with Broad Beans
Kusksu bil-Ful

Ingredients

280g (10oz) couscous (small pasta pellets)
1 onion chopped
140g (5oz) broad beans
85g (3oz) tomatoes peeled
57g (2oz) tomato paste
1 cube beef stock
1 l (32fl oz) water
1 tbsp olive oil

Method
1. Fry the chopped onion in the olive oil until it turns golden brown. Then add the tomatoes and tomato paste, stirring gently.
2. Add the water and bring to a boil.
3. Add the beef stock and couscous. Simmer until it is cooked.
4. Add the broad beans about 10 minutes before removing from the heat. Serve hot.

Mahi-Mahi Pie
Torta tal-Lampuki

Ingredients

1kg (35.25oz) mahi-mahi fish (*lampuki*)
1 onion sliced
2 tomatoes peeled and chopped
1 medium-sized cauliflower divided up
500g (17.5oz) spinach
8 olives
500g (17.5oz) flour
250g (8.75oz) shortening
2 tbsp olive oil
120ml (4fl oz) water
salt to taste

Method
1. Cut each mahi-mahi fish into 4 portions. Dip the portions in flour and fry them in the shortening until cooked through, but not overcooked. Remove the bones. Set aside while preparing the other ingredients.
2. Fry the onion in the olive oil until soft, then add the tomatoes.
3. Add the spinach and cauliflower, together with the water and salt to taste. Cover and simmer until the vegetables are soft. Add the olives and stir with a wooden spoon.
4. Line a 12" x 8" pie dish with a layer of pastry. Put half the vegetable mixture on it and place the fish portions on top. Cover these with a layer of the remaining vegetables, then cover everything with a pastry lid.
5. Bake for about 30 minutes on the middle shelf of a moderately preheated oven until the top is golden. Serve either hot with vegetables or cold.

Fried Cabbage with Eggs
Kaboċċi Moqlija bil-Bajd

Ingredients
1kg (35 oz) cabbage
3 eggs
50g (1.75oz) butter
grated Parmesan cheese
salt and pepper

Method
1. Wash and shred the cabbage, then boil it in salted water.
2. When cooked, drain the water.
3. Heat the butter and fry the cabbage for a few seconds.
4. Add the eggs and continue cooking for 10 minutes.
5. Serve hot with a generous dollop of Parmesan cheese.

Maltese Scrambled Eggs
Balbuljata

Ingredients
2 or 3 large tomatoes peeled and chopped
1 onion finely chopped
1 tbsp olive oil
50g (1.75oz) butter
chopped garlic to taste
1 tbsp parsley or mint chopped
8 eggs
salt and pepper

Method
1. Cook the onion in the olive oil and a little butter until it is soft. Add the garlic and tomatoes. Cook them for another 5 minutes until golden.
2. Beat the eggs lightly with the salt and pepper. Pour them on the tomatoes and onions, adding the remaining butter and parsley/mint.
3. Stir continuously over low heat until the eggs are set. Then stir them once over heat. Serve immediately.

Octopus
Qarnita

<u>Ingredients</u>
1kg (35.25oz) octopus
2 tbsp red wine
2 tbsp extra virgin olive oil
2 tbsp parsley chopped
2 cloves garlic finely chopped
1 tsp red pepper flakes
juice from 1 medium-sized lemon

<u>Method</u>
1. Clean and wash the octopus. Pat dry and do not cut up. Freeze the octopus for 3 days before cooking to ensure it does not become rubbery.
2. When ready to cook it, place the octopus in a deep pan, pour the red wine, and cover it. Bring it rapidly to a boil, then simmer it for 1.5 hours.
3. Turn the octopus over in the pan once or twice until the sides turn pink. Check for tenderness with a fork. If not sufficiently done, let the octopus simmer for about 10 minutes, checking it every 10 minutes after that.

<u>Dressing</u>
4. Mix the chopped parsley, finely chopped garlic, red pepper flakes, salt and pepper, olive oil, and lemon juice in a bowl with a wooden spoon.
5. Pour the dressing over the roughly chopped octopus and toss well. Serve either hot or cold.

Spaghetti with Anchovies
Spagetti bl-Inċova

Ingredients
480g (17oz) spaghetti
1 tbsp olive oil
3 cloves garlic chopped
12 anchovy fillets in oil
2 tbsp marjoram
3 tbsp fennel chopped
1 pot boiling water

Topping
200g (7oz) breadcrumbs
3 cloves garlic finely chopped
3 tbsp parsley chopped

Method
1. Fry the chopped garlic in olive oil until golden brown. Then add the anchovy fillets and dissolve them in the hot oil. Add the marjoram and fennel, stirring gently. Remove them all from the heat.
2. In a separate pan fry the breadcrumbs in olive oil. Then add the remaining garlic and parsley.
3. Boil the water in yet another pot and cook the spaghetti. When ready, drain the pasta into a separate bowl without rinsing the pasta and return the latter to the pot.
4. Add the garlic-and-anchovies mix and stir well. Then add the previously-drained water and stir again until everything is mixed.
5. Serve topped with fried breadcrumbs instead of cheese.

Spaghetti with Octopus
Spagetti bil-Qarnit

Ingredients
800g (28oz) octopus
1 kg (35.25oz) spaghetti
2 tbsp olive oil
3 onions chopped
10 black or brown olives
2 tbsp tomato purée
1 tsp sugar
3 large tomatoes chopped
1 tbsp capers
1 tbsp mint chopped
2 tbsp parsley chopped
1 tbsp bay leaf chopped
125ml (4.23fl oz) red wine
125ml (4.23fl oz) white wine
2 sizeable pots boiling water
salt and pepper

Method
1. Clean the octopus by turning its head inside out. Remove the intestines, beak, and eyes. Freeze it for at least 3 days before its intended cooking, otherwise it becomes rubbery if cooked fresh.
2. Place the octopus in a pot of boiling water that has already been salted and bring it once more to a boil. Then discard the water and cut the octopus into slices.
3. In another pot heat the olive oil. Fry the chopped onions and garlic until they become soft and golden. Then add the octopus and fry gently for another 3 minutes.

4. Add the red and white wine. Then bring everything to a boil on high heat. Stir well and cook for another 3 minutes.
5. Add the chopped tomatoes, tomato paste, salt and pepper to taste. Add the sugar and stir well. Cover the pot and simmer for 30 minutes.
6. Add the olives, capers, mint, parsley, and bay leaf. Simmer for another 30 minutes, stirring carefully with a wooden spoon.
7. Cook the spaghetti in boiling water, with salt to taste. Drain the water and place in plates. Do not rinse the pasta.
8. About 10 minutes before serving, uncover the pot with the octopus and turn up the heat to thicken the dish. Serve hot when ready.

Spinach and Tuna Pie
Torta tat-Tonn u l-Ispinaċi

Ingredients

500g (17.5oz) puff pastry
200g (7oz) tuna fish flakes or chunks
200g (7oz) ratatouille
2 kg (71oz) spinach chopped
6 anchovy fillets
12 olives chopped
1 cup cooked peas
1 large onion finely chopped
4 cloves garlic crushed
3 tbsp capers
4 tbsp olive oil
4 tbsp mint
2 tbsp tomato purée
salt and pepper

Method
1. Heat the olive oil. Fry the chopped onion and crushed garlic until golden in color.
2. Add all the other ingredients one by one and cook until every vegetable is well-baked. Do not leave any liquid in the pan. Cool the mixture before proceeding.
3. Roll out the puff pastry and line it in the bottom of an oven dish. Add the mixture and press it down into the pastry case. Cover with a pastry lid, seal the edges, and prick all over with a fork to let the air out.
4. Bake the pie at 200°C (400°F), gas mark 6, for about 45 minutes until golden brown. Make sure it settles and cools down. Serve at room temperature.

Spinach Lasagna
Lażanja tal-Ispinaċi

Ingredients

285g (10oz) spinach chopped
200g cottage cheese
1 box lasagna sheets
2 cups mozzarella cheese grated
1 egg beaten
1 tbsp basil
1 small onion
2 garlic cloves crushed
salt and pepper to taste

Method

1. Cook the spinach in a pot, then drain it out completely, pressing out any excess moisture that may be left. Set it aside in a large bowl.
2. Cook the lasagna sheets until they are semi-tender. Do not overcook. Preheat the oven to 177°C (350°F).
3. Process together with a wooden spoon the cottage cheese, salt and pepper, egg, mozzarella cheese, basil, garlic, and onion in a small bowl until the mixture is smooth.
4. Add #3 to the spinach and stir until everything is thoroughly combined.
5. Layer one-half of the cooked lasagna in a 9" x 13" baking pan. Pour the filling onto it and spread it evenly to the sides of the pan.
6. Place another layer of cooked lasagna on the filling and top with a sauce of your choice (red or white) and the remaining mozzarella cheese.
7. Bake for about 40 minutes. Serve hot.

Stuffed Green Peppers
Bżar Aħdar Ikkuppat

Ingredients
2 green peppers split, with seeds removed
250g (9oz) tuna fish
1 cup rice
2 tbsp green olives
2 tbsp capers
1 cup breadcrumbs[4]
juice of 1 lemon

Kapunata
2 tbsp olive oil
1 large onion chopped
4 potatoes sliced
2 tbsp fennel
salt and pepper

Method
1. Boil the rice in a pan until slightly soft. Do not overcook.
2. Mix the breadcrumbs, tuna fish, olives, capers, *kapunata*, salt and pepper, capers, and lemon juice in a bowl. Add the olive oil and mix everything together.
3. Add in the rice and mix well.
4. Stuff the green peppers with the above filling.
5. Spread the olive oil at the bottom of a baking dish, then layer in the onions and potatoes. Place the stuffed peppers on top.
6. Add any remaining potatoes around the edge of the dish.

---

[4] Cooked rice can be substituted for the breadcrumbs according to personal preference.

7. Sprinkle the potatoes with the fennel seeds. Add salt and pepper.
8. Add some water to cover the bottom of the dish before baking, so that the food does not dry up.
9. Cover the dish with aluminum foil and bake for 30 minutes.
10. Remove the foil and bake for yet another 30 minutes. Serve either hot or cold.

Stuffed Green Peppers with Mahi-Mahi
Bżar Aħdar Ikkuppat bil-Lampuki

Ingredients

4 large green peppers
25g (1oz) tomato purée
2 eggs
300g (11oz) mahi-mahi fish cooked
25g (1oz) green olives chopped
150g (5.5oz) cooked rice (white or brown)
1 tbsp parsley chopped
2 tbsp olive oil
50g (2oz) onions chopped
salt and pepper

Method

1. Remove the top and inside of the green peppers. Keep the tops.
2. Heat the olive oil and fry the onions in a pan until golden.
3. Add the tomato purée and a little water, simmering them for about 10 minutes.
4. Add the cooked rice, chopped olives, salt and pepper, cooked mahi-mahi fish, and chopped parsley.
5. Add the eggs and continue simmering for another 10 minutes.
6. Stuff the green peppers with the above mixture and replace the tops.
7. Bake in a moderate oven for about one hour. Serve hot or cold.

Stuffed Green Peppers with Tuna
Bżar Aħdar bit-Tonn taż-Żejt

Ingredients

4 large green peppers
150g (5.5oz) cooked rice (white or brown)
50g (2oz) onions chopped
25g (1oz) tomato purée
300g (11oz) tuna fish
2 eggs
25g (1oz) green olives chopped
1 tbsp parsley chopped
2 tbsp olive oil
salt and pepper

Method

1. Remove the top and inside of the green peppers. Keep the tops.
2. Heat the olive oil and fry the onions in a pan until golden.
3. Add the tomato purée and a little water, simmering them for about 10 minutes.
4. Add the cooked rice, chopped olives, salt and pepper, tuna fish, and chopped parsley.
5. Add the eggs and continue simmering for another 10 minutes.
6. Stuff the green peppers with the above mixture and replace the tops.
7. Bake in a moderate oven for about one hour. Serve hot or cold.

Stuffed Marrows
Qargha Baghli Kkuppat

Ingredients
1 kg (35.3oz) marrows
handful of parsley roughly chopped
2 tbsp garlic crushed
2 tbsp olive oil
salt and pepper to taste
little water

Method
1. Add all the ingredients in a pan. Simmer to a boil.
2. Turn the heat up and mash everything together. Let the water evaporate.
3. Serve hot or cold.

Tuna Fish Stew
Stuffat tat-Tonn

Ingredients

500g (18oz) tuna fish
2 tbsp olive oil
2 large onion chopped
2 garlic cloves crushed
4 tomatoes peeled and diced
200g (7oz) olives
50g (2oz) capers
white wine
salt and pepper to taste

Method

1. Cut the tuna into chunks and fry it with the olive oil in a pan. Then remove the tuna from the pan and keep it hot.
2. Chop the onions and fry them until tender. Add the garlic and tomatoes. Simmer everything until slightly cooked.
3. Add the olives and capers. Then add the fried tuna. Simmer again until thoroughly cooked.
4. Add a dash of white wine for flavor as the stew is simmering. Serve hot when done.

Fried Vermicelli Pie
Tarja bil-Bajd

Ingredients

600g (21oz) vermicelli pasta
4 eggs beaten
25g (1oz) butter
200g (7oz) grated Parmesan cheese
pan of water
salt and pepper to taste

Method
1. Cook the vermicelli pasta until slightly tender in a pan of water, then drain and discard the water. Do not overcook.
2. Mix together the beaten eggs and grated Parmesan cheese in a bowl. Season with salt and pepper.
3. Add in the cooked vermicelli and mix everything well together.
4. Fry the butter in a separate flat pan until it starts sizzling. Then fry the vermicelli for about 5 minutes until the bottom is golden.
5. Flip the vermicelli over and fry the other side until also golden.
6. Remove from the heat and serve.

5 – DRINKS

Carob Syrup
Ġulepp

Ingredients
1kg (35.3oz) carob pods
1kg (35.3oz) sugar (white or brown)
1 tsp cloves ground
water as needed
whisky to taste

Method
1. Wipe the carob pods clean, then wash them in 4 changes of water.
2. Roast them for about 10 minutes in one layer.
3. Let the carobs cool down, then break each pod into 4 pieces.
4. Soak them overnight in water.
5. Bring the carob pods to a boil in the same water on the following day, then simmer for 30 minutes.
6. Drain the water, pressing the pods to extract the maximum juice from them. Discard the pods.
7. Add the sugar and cloves to the carob juice. Boil it slowly for 30 minutes.
8. Cool the carob syrup down. Add a dash of whisky to taste.

Honeyed Wine
Imbid bl-Għasel

Ingredients
1 bottle white wine
4 tbsp clear honey
2 tbsp fresh mint

Method[5]
1. Gently warm 200ml (7fl oz) of white wine in a pan.
2. Add the honey and stir gently with a wooden spoon until incorporated.
3. Add the mint and allow to cool.
4. Remove the mint.
5. Mix in the remaining wine. Serve either hot (reheat briefly) or cold.

---

[5] Honeyed wine made this way is a 2000-year-old recipe.

Maltese Coffee
Kafè Malti Msajjar

Ingredients
5 tbsp ground coffee (blend of your choice)
1/2 tsp ground aniseed
1/2 tsp ground cloves
2 tsp roasted chicory
1 tsp honey or carob syrup
1/2 tsp orange rind grated
dark rum
water

Method
1. Mix together the ground coffee, roasted chicory, ground aniseed, and ground cloves in a small bowl.
2. Add the mixture to the funnel of an espresso pot with as much water as you need. Compress the coffee mix for a richer flavor and brew on low heat until it boils.
3. Add the honey or carob syrup to a mug and pour the coffee over it when ready, stirring continuously to dissolve. Then add the grated orange rind and a dash of dark rum.
4. Stir again and drink.

6 – PUDDINGS

Rice Pudding
Pudina tar-Ross

<u>Ingredients</u>
1/2 cup long grain rice cooked lightly
1/3 cup sugar (white or brown)
1/4 tsp salt
pinch nutmeg
2 cups milk
2/3 cup water
1 tbsp unsalted butter
1/2 tsp vanilla or cinnamon
1/3 cup raisins

<u>Method</u>
1. Preheat the oven to 150°C (300°F). Lightly grease a medium-sized baking dish.
2. Mix all the ingredients together except the raisins and place the mixture in the dish. Bake uncovered for about 1 hour.
3. Stir in the raisins, dust the top lightly with vanilla or cinnamon. Reduce the heat to 120°C (250°F) and bake for another 30 minutes. Serve hot or cold.

7 – DESSERTS

Deep Fried Dates
Imqaret

Ingredients
Pastry
650g (23oz) plain flour
175g (6oz) margarine
85g (3oz) sugar (white or brown)
1 egg beaten
vegetable oil
1 tsp baking powder

Filling
360g (13oz) dates pitted and chopped
1 orange rind grated
aniseed liqueur to taste
orange-blossom water

Method
1. Sift the flour and baking powder. Then rub the margarine into the flour until the mixture feels like breadcrumbs. Add the sugar and mix well. sugar.
2. Bind the mixture with the egg to make the dough. Let it set for about 30 minutes.
3. Add the ingredients of the filling into a pan and cook them over low heat, stirring occasionally. Simmer until the mix becomes creamy. Then remove from heat and place in a bowl, leaving it to cool off.
4. Roll out the dough on a floured surface in a 10cm-(4")-wide strip. Moisten its edges and spoon the filling down the

middle, folding the dough to enclose the filling. Press the edges together so that the filling does not fall out.

5. Cut the dough diagonally into 5cm (2") long diamond-shaped *imqaret* with a sharp knife.
6. Deep fry the *imqaret* in boiling oil until golden brown.
7. Drain thoroughly and serve hot.

Hard Carob Sweets
Karamelli tal-Ħarrub[6]

<u>Ingredients</u>
carob syrup
water

<u>Method</u>
1. Boil the carob syrup in a pan over high heat. Stir continuously until it dissolves and becomes caramelized to a hard-crack stage.
2. Pour the mix onto a marble surface. Let it cool and cut the caramelized mix into small squares.
3. Wrap the squares in grease-proof paper to avoid stickiness.

---

[6] *Karamelli tal-Ħarrub* are very popular in the Maltese Islands during Passion Week.

Hot Cross Buns

Ingredients
2 tsp dried yeast
500g (18oz) plain flour
90g (3oz) sugar (white or brown)
300ml (10fl oz) milk
1 tbsp vegetable oil
1 tsp salt
1 tsp cinnamon
1/2 tsp spice of one's choice
1/4 tsp nutmeg grated
60g (2oz) butter
1 large egg beaten
140g (5oz) sultanas (or mixed currants, sultanas, raisins)
30g (1oz) mixed peel

Crosses
2 tbsp flour
2 tbsp cold water
glaze
4 tbsp sugar
1/4 tsp cinnamon
150ml (5fl oz) boiling water

Method
1. Sift the flour, spice, salt, and yeast to evenly distribute them.
2. Heat the milk in a pan over low temperature and melt the butter in it.
3. Add the milk and butter mix to the flour and remix thoroughly. Then add the beaten egg and mix everything

together to form the dough, working in the dried fruit and peel.
4. Knead the dough on a flat lightly-floured surface until it feels smooth.
5. Add the vegetable oil to a bowl, then place the dough in it, covering it with wrap. Leave in a warm place until the dough is double in size.
6. Punch the dough down, then separate it into 12 buns.
7. Place the buns on a baking tray. Cover and allow them to rise once again until double in size.
8. *To make the crosses*, mix the flour and water to form a thick paste. Then spoon this paste into a *Ziplock* bag, cut out a little hole in the corner, and pipe the mixture in crosses on top of the buns. Bake the crossed buns at 220°C (392°F) for about 20 minutes.
9. *To make the glaze*, mix all the listed ingredients together and dissolve the sugar in the boiling water.
10. Brush over the buns while still hot and serve.

Kwareżimal[7]

Ingredients
500g (18oz) almonds ground
300g (11oz) brown sugar
30g (1oz) cocoa powder
1 tbsp rice flour
150g (5.5oz) plain flour
2 egg whites
2 tbsp water
3 tbsp anisette
1 tbsp orange-blossom water
1 tsp mixed spices of one's choice
1 tsp orange rind grated
1 tsp lemon rind grated
juice of 1 orange

Topping
1/2 roasted hazelnuts crushed
1/2 cup honey

Method
1. Add the egg whites, water, lemon and orange rinds, orange-blossom water, orange juice, anisette, and sugar to a large bowl. Stir well with a fork.
2. Add the almonds, flour, cocoa powder, rice flour, and mixed spices. Continue stirring until all the ingredients form a thick paste. Preheat the oven to 175°C (347°F).

---

[7] *Kwareżimal* is a recipe developed by the Knights of Malta. It is called *kwareżimal* because it refers to the *quaresima*, the 40 days of Lent.

3. Line the baking tray with baking paper, then moisten your hands with a little water. Take heaped tablespoons of the above mixture and form into 12cm (5") rolls, arranging them on the tray and gently flattening them out.
4. Dip a knife in the water and make X dents across the top of the rolls.
5. Bake them for 25 minutes, then remove the *kwareżimal* from the heat.
6. Drizzle the *kwareżimal* generously with honey and sprinkle them with the crushed nuts. Serve or store them in an airtight container.

Maltese Nougat
Qubbajt

Ingredients
800g (28oz) white sugar
300g (11oz) roasted almonds
edible rice paper sheets as needed
1 tsp cinnamon
1 tbsp vegetable oil
250ml (8.5fl oz) water

Method
1. Oil a shallow baking tray and line it with a sheet of rice paper.
2. Dissolve the sugar in the water in a heavy pan over low heat, shaking (not stirring) it to a boil, until it turns into hot syrup.
3. Grease lights a slab of marble with the vegetable oil mixed with water. Then spread the almonds over it and sprinkle the cinnamon.
4. Pour the syrup on #3 and work the mixture with two spatulas. When everything starts to harden, spoon the mix into the rice paper case and let it cool. Serve when completely hardened.

Treacle Rings
Qagħaq tal-Għasel

Ingredients
Filling
600g (21oz) treacle
150g (5.3oz) sugar
75g (2.7oz) jam
zest of lemon, orange, tangerine

Dough
600g (21oz) flour
2 egg yolks
750ml (25.5fl oz) water
50g (2oz) candied peel finely chopped
250g (9oz) semolina
pinch of ground cloves
50g (2oz) margarine
little water
baking sheets

Method
1. Add the filling ingredients, except the semolina, to a pan and bring to a boil.
2. Thicken with semolina, adding a little at a time.
3. Cook for a few seconds and let it cool. Rub the margarine into the flour and bind everything with the yolks and water.
4. Let the dough set for two hours, then roll it out into strips of 8cm by 15cm (3" x 6").

5. Put some filling in the middle of the dough throughout its whole length. Then bring the ends of the dough together to form a ring.
6. Sprinkle a baking sheet with semolina and place the rings on the sheet.
7. Lash the dough in several different places with a sharp knife so that the treacle filling shows.
8. Bake the rings in a moderately-hot oven for 25 minutes. Serve after having let them cool down to room temperature.

8 – COOKIES

Bitter Almond Biscuits
Biskuttini tal-Lewż Morr

Ingredients
400g (14oz) almonds ground
400g (14oz) castor sugar
4 egg whites beaten
25ml (1fl oz) almond essence
edible rice paper as needed
whole almonds

Method
1. Mix all the ingredients together until the sugar disappears and the mixture becomes sticky to the touch.
2. Roll the mixture into small balls, then place them on a pan over rice paper.
3. Insert a sliced blanched almond in the top of each ball.
4. Bake the balls at 180°C (356°F) for 15 minutes, the remove from the oven and let them cool down.[8]
5. Serve at room temperature or store in an air-tight container.

---

[8] If you like them hard, rather than soft, let the balls bake for about 30 minutes, making sure they do not get burned.

Crunchy Maltese Rusks
Biskuttelli

Ingredients
15g (0.5oz) yeast
175ml (6fl oz) water
400g (14oz) flour
pinch of salt
50g (2oz) butter
1 tsp aniseed crushed
200g (7oz) castor sugar

Method
1. Cream the yeast in water, sieve the flour and salt it into a bowl.
2. Mix in the butter. Then, making a well, add the sugar and aniseed.
3. Add the yeast and water.
4. Bring the mixture together, then turn it onto a work surface and knead until a pliable bread like dough results.
5. Return the bread to the bowl, cover it, and let it set in a warm place until doubled in bulk.
6. Knead the dough briefly to knock it back, then form into 4 elongated cakes.
7. Bake on a tray at 200°C (400°F), gas mark 6, until they are cooked through.
8. Let the cakes cool overnight. Then cut each cake into wafer-thin slices, laying them out again on a tray.
9. Bake the slices at 180°C (350°F), gas mark 4, until crisp and golden. Let them cool on a wire rack. Serve at room temperature or store in an airtight container.

Hard Thin Biscuits
Galletti

Ingredients
1kg (35oz) flour
1 tsp salt
50g (2oz) yeast
1 tsp sugar
60g (2.12oz) butter melted
warm water

Method
1. Dissolve the yeast and sugar in a cup of warm water until the mixture becomes frothy.
2. Mix the flour and salt in a large bowl. Then add the melted butter and mix again.
3. Add the yeast mixture to #2 and mix everything well. Add warm water as needed to ensure consistency of the dough.
4. Knead the dough on a flat surface, then place it in a large bowl and cover it. Let the dough to rest for 1 hour.
5. Knead the dough again and cut it into small portions.
6. Roll out the portions as thinly as possible and cut them into small circles with a scone cutter.
7. Put the circles on a lightly dusted oven tray and bake until golden brown. Let them cool. Serve at room temperature or store in an airtight container.

Village Biscuits
Biskuttini tar-Raħal

Ingredients
3 eggs beaten
pinch of cinnamon and ground cloves
230g (8oz) sugar
1 tsp baking powder
460g (16oz) flour
orange-blossom water
1 tsp spice of own choice
milk as needed

Method
1. Add the sugar to the eggs and beat them together.
2. Mix the baking powder with the flour and add the spice. Then add this mixture to #1.
3. Form into dough and add the orange-blossom water. If the dough feels stiff, soften it with a little milk.
4. Form the mixture into round biscuit shapes and place them on a lightly floured tray. Bake them in a moderately hot oven until pale golden-brown. Then remove them from the heat and let them cool.
5. Let the biscuits harden by being exposed to room temperature air overnight. Serve or store in an airtight container.

9 – EASTER FARE

Rabbit with Vermouth
Fenek bil-Vermut

Ingredients
1kg (35oz) rabbit chopped
1kg (35oz) potatoes
1 bottle *Vermouth*
4 large onions sliced
2 tbsp bay leaves
200g (7oz) carrots chopped
200g (7oz) peas
200g (7oz) zucchini sliced into rings
3 garlic cloves
2 tbsp olive oil
1 tbsp sesame crushed
1 tsp curry powder
water as needed
salt and pepper to taste

Method
1. Soak the rabbit overnight in the red wine together with salt and pepper, the sliced onions, and 1 tbsp bay leaves.
2. Layer the bottom of an appropriately-sized baking tray with the onions and 2 garlic cloves, sprinkling them with the remaining tbsp of bay leaves.
3. Slice the potatoes into thick rounds and place them on the layer of onions and garlic, sprinkling them with olive oil, salt and pepper, the crushed sesame, and curry powder. Bake in a hot oven until the top of the potatoes is scrunchy and golden brown.

4. Fry the chopped rabbit in a little olive oil in a pan on low heat in a pan to retain its flavor. When almost ready, add 1 garlic clove and stir thoroughly until cooked.
5. Add the rabbit to the potatoes in the baking tray, covering it with *Vermouth*. Let it set for about 15 minutes.
6. Add the carrots, peas, and zucchini on the sides of the rabbit. Cover everything again in a thin layer of *Vermouth* and bake for about 30 minutes or until the rabbit meat can easily be pulled away from its bones by a fork.
7. Remove from the heat and serve hot.

Almonds Pie
Torta tal-Lewż

Ingredients
Dough
400g (14oz) flour
1/2 tsp baking powder
190g (7oz) margarine
120g (4oz) castor sugar
juice and rind of 1 orange thinly chopped
1 egg yolk beaten
1/2 tsp vanilla

Filling
600g (21oz) icing sugar
600g (21oz) almonds ground
8 eggs beaten
1/2 tsp vanilla
rind of 3 lemons thinly chopped

Method
1. Sift the flour and baking powder.
2. Add the sugar and margarine, rubbing them all together until it a crumb-like dough is formed.
3. Add the orange rind and juice, egg yolk, and vanilla. Mix everything into a smooth dough. Place in the fridge and let it set overnight.
4. Line a baking tray with the dough.
5. Mix all the filling ingredients together in a large bowl and spoon them into the dough with a wooden spoon.
6. Cover the filling with a dough cover and bake at 150°C (302°F) for 1.25 hours or until the top has turned golden.

Shaped Almonds Easter Cake
Figolla tal-Għid

Ingredients
Dough
350g (12oz) castor sugar
800g (28oz) flour
400g (14oz) butter
rind of 1 lemon grated
4 egg yolks beaten
honey
almonds as needed

Almond Paste
600g (21oz) castor sugar
3 egg whites beaten
rind of 1 lemon grated
orange-blossom water
600g (21oz) almonds ground

Finish
glacé icing
royal icing
small chocolate easter egg

Method
1. Mix the flour with the sugar for the pastry, then rub in butter until the mixture looks as though it is fine crumbs.
2. Add the egg yolks and grated lemon rind, then mix a little water to get a workable dough. Let the mixture chill.
3. Add the lemon rind and orange-blossom water to the almonds. Bind them with egg whites.

4. Roll out the pastry mix and cut out two identical shapes of it, one for the top, one for the bottom.
5. Lay out the first shape on a greased baking tray and spread the almond paste on it, leaving a small margin. Then place the second shape on the paste and press the edges together, wetting them with a small brush to ensure binding.
6. Bake at 200°C/400°F for five minutes. Then bake again at 180°C/350°F for about 20 minutes until pale golden. Let the *figolla* cool down on the tray.
7. Coat the top shape with the glacé icing, then decorate it with some royal icing in a different color according to taste. While the icing is soft, insert a foil-wrapped egg into the *figolla*, then finish with some ground almonds.

Note: The traditional shapes of *figolli* are men, women, fish, and baskets. The chocolate Easter egg is wrapped in bright colors.

Royal / Glacé Icing
100g (4oz) icing sugar sieved
2 tbsp (30ml) water
flavor to taste
coloring to taste

Method
1. Place the sieved icing sugar in a bowl. Add the water and coloring. Beat until smooth and thick enough to coat the back of a spoon.
2. If the mixture is too thin, add more icing sugar. If it is too thick, add more water a few drops at a time.

Saint Joseph's Fritters
Zeppoli ta' San Ġużepp

Ingredients
Choux Dough
500g (18oz) flour
packet of margarine
1/2 tsp salt
1 tsp yeast
1 tsp baking powder
1 tbsp sugar
4 large eggs beaten
warm water

Filling
500g (18oz) ricotta cheese
vanilla essence
90g (3oz) granulated sugar
20g (0.7oz) candied peel diced
20g (0.7oz) roasted almonds chopped
20g (0.7oz) dark chocolate chopped

Topping
drizzle of honey
roasted almonds chopped

Method
1. Mix the flour and salt.
2. Cut the margarine into cubes and knead with flour until the mixture looks like breadcrumbs.

3. Melt the yeast in a glass with a little warm water. Then make a hole in the middle of the flour, pour in the melted yeast and knead.
4. Keep adding a little warm water as needed. Then cover and let the mixture set for two hours.
5. Mix the ricotta cheese with all the other ingredients for the filling. Beat in the eggs one by one depending on the density of the mixture, so that it does not become too liquid.
6. Cut the choux dough into sizeable portions and open them up with a wooden rolling pin.
7. Add a spoonful of filling onto each portion and close the dough.
8. Brush the egg yolks onto the pastry and bake in a hot oven until golden. Then remove and sprinkle with the roasted almonds. Serve when cool.

www.ingramcontent.com/pod-product-compliance
Lightning Source LLC
Chambersburg PA
CBHW071125030426
42336CB00013BA/2210